REDEMPTION

REDEMPTION
Alister McGrath

Fortress Press
Minneapolis

REDEMPTION

First Fortress Press Edition 2006

Scripture quotations are from the New Revised Standard Version of the Bible, copyright © 1989 by the Division of Christian Education of the National Council of the Churches of Christ in the USA and used by permission.

The Prodigal's Return by Sir Edward John Poynter (1836–1919),
Private Collection, © The Fine Art Society, London, UK/Bridgeman Art Library.
Cover and interior design and typesetting: Theresa Maynard

ISBN: 0-8006-3702-X

Manufactured in Belgium

09   08   07   06   1   2   3   4   5   6   7   8   9   10

contents

introduction

The New Testament is saturated with the belief that something *new* has happened because of Jesus of Nazareth. In some way, the life, death and resurrection of Jesus Christ have changed the way things are, changed the way we see things, and begun a process of transformation and renewal. The absolute conviction and recognition that something (dare we say everything?) has changed on account of Christ is central to the New Testament's joyful proclamation and celebration of the gospel.

What is it that has changed so radically? How are these changes anchored to the history of Jesus of Nazareth? How are we to visualize the difference that Christ's death and resurrection have made? What ideas, images or concepts can we use to clarify their meaning and appreciate their importance? Theology is about intellectual mapping, about giving an account of the landscape of faith. And when theology comes to try to survey and represent this particular territory, it finds that it is vastly more expansive than our limited minds can fully embrace. Christians have always needed a very large repertoire of metaphors to deal with such a rich, multilayered reality. It turns out to be much easier to provide a set of snapshots than to produce a detailed map of the terrain.

The New Testament provides us with an album of such images. Some are drawn from the cultic system of the Old Testament, speaking of the death of Jesus in terms of a sacrifice or offering to God. Others are drawn from the cultural world of the New Testament period: purchasing the freedom of a bondsman, liberating someone from captivity, wiping the slate clean, healing someone's wounds, being declared innocent before one's accusers – all are seen as aspects of the greater whole that we call 'redemption'. The task set for Christian theology is to integrate these ideas, putting these snapshots together so that they disclose something of the greater panorama of redemption. Limits on space mean that all we can hope to achieve in this volume is to explore some of them, leaving their correlation to other, more detailed, studies.

Why is it so important and helpful to investigate these ideas? I have long found that a phrase I first encountered when beginning to study theology at Oxford University in 1977 is helpful at this point. It comes from the writings of the German Lutheran Phillipp Melanchthon: 'To know Christ is to know his benefits.' These words, written in 1521, suggest that our understanding and appreciation of Christ are intensified by focusing on what he has done for us – the difference that he has made. We can deepen our grasp of who Christ *is* by reflecting on what he has *achieved*.

So what difference does Jesus make? How does he change the way in which we see the world, think about God and ourselves, cope with suffering and loneliness, and live out the good life? In a short volume such as this, we can only hope to begin to consider some of these many themes. We shall use a series of evocative images to help us recreate and re-enact the final events of the earthly life of Christ, combining theological reflection on what Jesus of Nazareth achieved with a more devotional emphasis on its costliness, and its impact upon us. Properly understood, the pivotal events of Passiontide engage our minds and our hearts, as we long to understand what is going on, while at the same time coming to terms with the disturbing fact that the Son of God died – and believed that he *had* to die – in order to transform our situation.

So let us begin to explore the loving purposes of God in bringing fallen humanity back to his tender embrace and how this connects with the final days of the life of Jesus of Nazareth.

Alister McGrath

being wanted

being wanted

In 1749, John Byrom, the inventor of a noted shorthand system, made his daughter a Christmas present of a song he had just composed. His 'Hymn for Christmas Day' is now known as 'Christians awake, salute the happy morn'. It affirms the link between incarnation and redemption and stresses the importance of holding both in mind, while reflecting on their significance.

> Oh, may we keep and ponder in our mind
> God's wondrous love in saving lost mankind!
> Trace we the Babe, who hath retrieved our loss,
> From His poor manger to His bitter cross,
> Tread in His steps, assisted by His grace,
> Till man's first heavenly state again takes place.

It is a fitting introduction to this book, which deals with the wonderful gospel proclamation of the redemption of humanity through Christ.

Yet this great act of divine redemption does not come out of the blue, as a solitary bolt of lightning flashing across an otherwise clear sky. The New Testament is emphatic: the God who redeems us in Christ is the same God who created the world, called Israel to be his people, and delivered Israel from slavery in Egypt and then again from exile in Babylon. God's act of redemption in Christ is a still-greater extension of his great acts of deliverance in the past. To understand the redemption that Christ achieves, we must trace its roots back to the dealings of God with Israel.

When Israel declared her faith in the Lord as her redeemer, she was bearing witness to her long history of experience of God's acts of redemption. The exodus from Egypt and the return from exile in Babylon are regularly proclaimed as acts of redemption, things that God has done to secure the safety and well-being of his people. The Psalmist invited

Israel to praise her God, who had redeemed his people with his strong arm (Psalm 77.15).

The New Testament reaffirms this divine action and initiative yet insists that these are funnelled through and focused on the person of Jesus of Nazareth. For the New Testament, as for the Church down the ages, Jesus is the 'mathematical point' (Martin Luther) at which the presence and activity of God in the world are concentrated. Yes, God is active and present throughout his creation; yet that presence and activity are seen in a definitive, unique way in the person of Jesus of Nazareth.

In another volume in this series, *Incarnation*, we showed how the Christian Church slowly but surely explained this divine involvement in terms of the incarnation of God in Christ. The last Old Testament prophet ends his vision of the future actions of God with this promise: 'The Lord whom you seek will suddenly come to his temple' (Malachi 3.1). The God who promised, through the great Old Testament prophets, to visit and redeem his people, did precisely that through coming to dwell among them in Jesus. God entered into our situation in order to transform it. Far from demanding that we raise ourselves to heaven, he came down from heaven in order to bring us there himself.

Even the name of the central figure of the Christian faith emphasizes this point. Remember, Mary and Joseph were not allowed to choose a name for their child; they were told what to call him – Jesus. 'You will call him "Jesus", for he will save his people from their sins' (Matthew 1.21). This rich, evocative name includes within itself a central theme of the gospel. For the name means 'God saves'. In the coming of Jesus, God has *acted*. God *sends* Jesus of Nazareth as the Saviour of humanity. The same God who acted to create humanity now acts again to redeem us and lead us through the gates of the New Jerusalem.

So what does redemption mean? Defining words is always problematic. To define is to limit, to restrict. At times, this can be helpful. We have all found ourselves in situations where a discussion has got nowhere for the very simple reason that people don't agree on what they mean by a word. Words like 'democracy', 'nature', 'freedom' and 'justice' mean different things to different people. Limiting a word's meaning is often necessary before a debate gets anywhere.

But what if a word is so rich, so complex, that we actually distort its significance by restricting it in this way, or by insisting that a word with many meanings or levels of significance can bear only one of them? Imagine the famous experiment carried out by Sir Isaac Newton at Trinity College, Cambridge, in the late seventeenth century. Newton passed a beam of white light through a glass prism and noticed that it emerged broken down into a spectrum of colours – red, orange, yellow, green, blue, indigo and violet. All those colours are already present in white light; the prism simply allowed the colours to be seen by separating them. Exactly the same thing, of course, can be seen in one of nature's greatest wonders – the rainbow.

The idea of redemption is like a seemingly simple beam of white light. Yet it is actually complex, composed of many elements, each of which needs to be identified and respected in its own right. It is a spiritual diamond with many facets, each of which needs to be seen, valued and appreciated. It might make life a lot easier if we defined redemption very tightly. But that would be like limiting the colours of the rainbow to green. How can we do this when there is so much more that needs to be said? One of the central tasks of theology is to unpack the treasures of the Christian gospel, so that they can be individually examined and valued. Theology is like Newton's prism, resolving the components of the gospel to help us identify, understand and appreciate them.

So what happens if we try to analyse the concept of redemption in this way? As might be expected, we come up with a rich range of meanings and associations, each of which casts light on a specific aspect of the Christian gospel. Our appreciation of the whole depends upon being able to identify and treasure its individual parts.

Perhaps the most basic meaning of the concept of 'redemption' is 'buying back' – as in the practice of redeeming slaves, a familiar event in New Testament times. At that time, people often sold themselves into slavery, sometimes for fixed periods, to raise much-needed funds for their family. A slave could redeem himself by buying his freedom. The Greek word used to describe this process could literally be translated as 'being taken out of the forum [i.e. the slave market]'. The fundamental idea here is of restoring someone to a state of liberty, with the emphasis laid upon liberation rather than upon the means used to achieve it. In the Old Testament, God is often said to redeem his people (see Deuteronomy 7.8; 2 Samuel 7.23; Hosea 7.13; Zechariah 10.8). Again, the emphasis falls on the act of divine deliverance or liberation rather than upon its financial basis (Isaiah 52.3 even makes it clear that money is not involved).

The New Testament sometimes uses the term to mean 'liberated from bondage' – for example, bondage to the law (Galatians 3.13; 4.5). More often, however, the word is used in a more general sense – simply being set free (Revelation 5.9; 14.3–4). Christ's death and resurrection are understood to set us free from bondage to sin and death. Paul's repeated emphasis that Christians are slaves who have been 'bought with a price' (1 Corinthians 6.20; 7.23) reminds us of the costliness of that redemption.

One of the most moving poetic accounts of this point is found in George Herbert's poem 'Redemption'. The imagery of the poem presents the 'redemption of the world' in terms of the costly purchase of a piece of land.

The poem skilfully invites us to join Herbert as he seeks this rich Lord in this new purchase. Where would he find him, he reasons, other than in the most cultivated and elegant surroundings? Yet, to his astonishment, he finds this rich Lord debased and wounded, surrounded by the lowly, criminals and outcasts. Is this what his rich Lord came to purchase? Is this humiliation, pain, and degradation what redemption entails?

> Having been tenant long to a rich Lord,
> Not thriving, I resolved to be bold,
> And make a suit unto Him, to afford
> A new small-rented lease, and cancel th'old.
>
> In heaven at His manor I Him sought:
> They told me there, that He was lately gone
> About some land, which he had dearly bought
> Long since on Earth, to take possession.
>
> I straight return'd, and knowing His great birth,
> Sought Him accordingly in great resorts –
> In cities, theatres, gardens, parks, and courts:

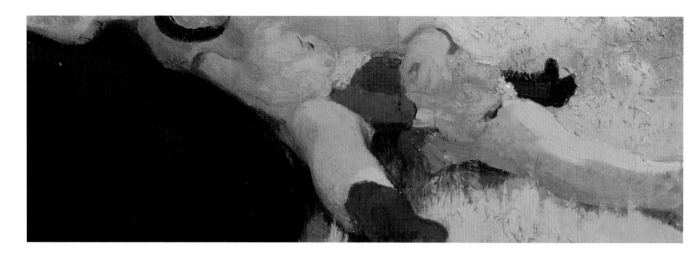

At length I heard a ragged noise and mirth
Of thieves and murderers; there I Him espied,
Who straight, 'Your suit is granted,' said, and died.

Herbert's language and imagery need a little time to percolate into our minds and imaginations. Sometimes more visual imagery is better able to achieve a direct connection with our imaginations. With this point in mind, we may turn to explore another aspect of redemption. One of Paul's ways of explaining the difference that Christ makes to humanity is that of *adoption* (Romans 8.15, 23; Galatians 4.5; Ephesians 1.5). It is a rich image, evoking one of the most profound human emotions and aspirations – the longing to belong somewhere. Interestingly, it is a notion derived from Roman, not Jewish, law, which Paul uses in explaining the benefits of the gospel to a Gentile readership.

Adoption is about being wanted. It is a compelling affirmation of belonging. Adopted people are transferred from a relational wasteland and welcomed into a family. They enter the family home, but not as uninvited strangers or interlopers who must constantly fear discovery, exposure and expulsion. The adopted are there by invitation of the head of the family, because they have been chosen. They are wanted. They are not gatecrashers into the kingdom of God, but are his welcome guests. They can luxuriate in the security and warmth of the family home, knowing that they have the right to be there. And having received this legal status of being adopted, they can call God 'Abba' – Father! – because that is what God has now become to them (Romans 8.15).

Something of the intimacy of this notion can be appreciated from the paintings of the Italian artist Amedeo Bocchi (1883–1976), many of whose works depict scenes of family life. His masterpiece *On the Lawn* shows a mother and daughter sheltering from the heat of the day beneath a parasol. There is no action taking place whatsoever. The mother tenderly embraces her daughter, who in turn firmly grasps her doll. The picture freezes a moment of acceptance and warmth. The daughter knows that she belongs there; that she is safe, enfolded in her mother's arms. How many of us have needed to hear words like this at critical moments in our lives: 'It's all right; I am here'? We might think, for example, of Jesus stilling the storm and giving the terrified disciples that same reassurance: 'Take heart, it is I; do not be afraid' (Mark 6.50).

What is the broader context? Where exactly is this lawn? What lies beyond the picture's margins? We have no idea. The threat of war may loom. Troops may be on the move. Economic recession may have gripped the nation. Yet here, frozen by the artist, is an image of personal security and acceptance. Whatever the context may be, this child is enfolded and protected. She is loved, accepted, and wanted.

As Western society fragments, losing its traditional family support structures, the need to belong somewhere becomes acutely important. People feel the need to belong, yet simultaneously feel that they do not belong anywhere. Where can they go? Who wants them? Who will accept them for what they are? Yet we are not speaking of a mere passive acceptance here. Rather, we are daring to speak of a love that cannot leave broken, wounded people as they are, but wants to heal them, to enable them to become something still better. And that is what redemption encompasses: an acceptance of what we are, on account of Christ, and the beginning of the process of healing and restoration.

That is what the Church is meant to be – the community that accepts and welcomes those who have already been accepted and welcomed by God. It is, as Augustine of Hippo often pointed out, like a hospital that receives the wounded to tend them, so that they might become whole again: even more so, that they might become what God wants them to be, rather than what they were forced to be through living in a fallen, broken world. Acceptance and love precede renewal and recovery. Redemption, in its deepest sense, is about being accepted as we are, while being transformed into what we are meant to be.

Lord, help us to know your peace in this disordered and dangerous world, and to know you as our shepherd as we journey in hope.

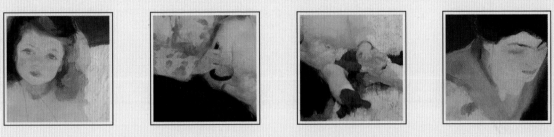

coming home

coming home

One of the best-loved Christian prayers is used at the beginning of the Service of Nine Lessons and Carols, originally developed at King's College, Cambridge, in the years immediately after the First World War, and now used throughout the world. The college chaplain at that time, Eric Milner-White, realized that something had to be done to make the Christmas story accessible and intelligible to a post-war generation that felt increasingly disconnected from church life. This famous opening 'Bidding Prayer' introduces the service of readings and carols, offering a framework that gives them both structure and meaning. It begins by setting the scene for the service, so familiar and yet constantly needing restatement.

> Beloved in Christ, be it this Christmas Eve our care and delight to prepare ourselves to hear again the message of the angels: in heart and mind to go even unto Bethlehem and see this thing which is come to pass, and with the Magi adore the Child lying in his Mother's arms.

One phrase in the prayer is often singled out for its verbal beauty and theological insight:

> Let us read and mark in Holy Scripture the tale of the loving purposes of God from the first days of our disobedience unto the glorious Redemption brought us by this Holy Child.

The point being made here is of such importance that it is easy to miss it. A 'tale' – a *story* – is being told and its two chief landmarks identified. Whatever else the Christmas story may mean, its fundamental sense is the transformation of the human situation through Christ. The long, complex and wonderful story set out in the pages of Scripture, when rightly

interpreted, discloses a loving God's quest to find a lost humanity and restore them to his tender care.

When rightly interpreted. Every story needs interpretation. What does it *mean*? The parables that Jesus told illustrate this point perfectly. Jesus told stories. While some saw their meaning immediately, others found them obscure and impenetrable or only discerned their surface meaning. Yes, Jesus told a very interesting story about a man sowing seed. And, yes, we all know that some of that seed didn't grow properly, because it fell on rocky ground, got eaten by birds or choked by weeds. What's that got to do with anything about God?

No wonder Jesus stressed the need for discernment to grasp the meaning of the parables. As he said to his disciples, 'To you has been given the secret of the kingdom of God, but for those outside, everything comes in parables; in order that "they may indeed look, but not perceive, and may indeed listen, but not understand"' (Mark 4.11–12). These stories have to be interpreted correctly, otherwise they conceal their true meaning, drawing down a veil over the secrets of the Kingdom of God, leaving people baffled, perhaps even irritated. What on earth has the growth of seeds got to do with the mysterious ways of God or the identity and mission of Jesus of Nazareth?

Luke's Gospel includes three parables, grouped together, which vividly illuminate the nature of redemption. What was lost has been found; the situation has been restored to what it ought to be, with rejoicing on all sides. The first such parable concerns a man who loses a sheep (Luke 15.4–7). What can he do but go out in search of it? And when he has found it, carry it home on his shoulders? And when he returns, celebrate his joy with his neighbours? The implication of the parable for an understanding of redemption is evident: when any of his creatures, whom he has created for fellowship with him, is lost, God searches for them, until finally, finding

them, he tenderly carries them home. It is a parable of incarnation (the shepherd going into the wilderness, which is where the lost sheep is to be found) and redemption (finding, returning, and restoring the lost).

The second such parable centres on a woman, clearly a person of independent means, who loses one of ten coins (Luke 15.8–10). Western male biblical interpreters have often assumed that the woman had been given the coins by her husband, or that the coins were some kind of ornamental jewellery. But the text neither demands nor permits any such interpretation. The woman owns ten coins in her own right, and loses one. Again, she rejoices when she finds the lost one, and the situation is restored. Each coin matters to her.

It is, however, the third of this group of parables that has attracted the most attention – so much attention, in fact, that it has become one of the best-known of all the parables. The parable of the Prodigal Son (Luke 15.11–32) tells of a father with two sons. We are not told why, but the younger demands to be given his share of the family fortune so that he can make his own way in the world. Kenneth Bailey, a writer with wide experience of Middle Eastern culture, remarks on the outrage that this demand would evoke. To demand an inheritance, here and now, is tantamount to wishing that the father were dead! Jesus' audience would immediately be hostile to this wayward son. How disrespectful! The father would be perfectly justified in throwing him out of the family home, and banishing him forever. Yet there is no hint of this. The son goes into exile by his own free choice. He banishes himself, while believing he has secured his freedom.

For the son wants his autonomy. He longs to make his own decisions, to be the master of his own destiny. To the intellectual historian, there is an uncanny parallel between the younger son of this parable, and the dominant mood of the Enlightenment. Humanity has come of age, and can dispense with God. Without him, we can achieve our own goals and destinies. We can manage very well on our own, without the nauseating heavenly paternalism of God.

Except it just doesn't work out like that. The son fritters away his inheritance (the word 'prodigal' has the sense of 'profligate'), and finds himself having to eke out a precarious existence as a swineherd. Even the pigs seem to manage better than he does. The proud master has become a pathetic slave, reduced to the level of an animal. It is unlikely that Jesus' audience would have felt in the least bit sorry for him. 'Serves him right!' 'That'll teach him!'

Yet this lack of sympathy on the audience's part does not invalidate the son's change of heart. A decision – a humiliating decision – is reached (Luke 15.18–19):

> I will get up and go to my father, and I will say to him, 'Father, I have sinned against heaven and before you; I am no longer worthy to be called your son; treat me like one of your hired hands.'

The son can no longer deny the reality of his situation. He has failed himself. He has learned that he lacks the wisdom, the strength and the resources to manage for himself. He needs to return to his father. Yet can he hope to be accepted back into the family home on any terms? Will he really belong there? (Again, we find the importance of the belonging and acceptance themes that we noted when considering the idea of adoption in the previous chapter.)

Suddenly, it is the father who is at the centre of the narrative. What will he do? How will he react when he is told that his son has crawled back home in disgrace? Jesus' audience might well have anticipated the father's righteous indignation descending on his son, who would be cast into the outer darkness in disgrace for his insulting and inconsiderate behaviour. Yet the parable tells a very different story – a story of grace and compassion (Luke 15.20).

> But while he was still far off, his father saw him and was filled with compassion; he ran and put his arms around him and kissed him.

It is so easy to read this familiar passage without noticing the critical point. How could the father have seen the returning son, when he was still some distance away? Surely the father would have been busy with family affairs, managing the estate. Then, gradually, we realize the truth. The father has been waiting. He has been watching from the flat roof of his house, in order to be able to see further, awaiting the return of his son from the far country of his self-imposed exile.

The pathos of the occasion is captured superbly by Sir Edward Poynter (1836–1919). In *The Prodigal's Return* (1869), Poynter depicts the father embracing the son. The contrast between the two figures could not be greater. The father, dressed in sumptuous clothing, soft sandals on his feet, a ring on his finger; the son, barefoot, dressed in rags. Above the father's head

we see the steps leading up to his observation point. How long, we wonder, had he been waiting for his son? The parable gives no indication of time. It might have been months; it might have been years. Yet the father was there, waiting, longing for the return of his son. Wayward he might have been; but he never ceased to be his son.

The feature of Poynter's *The Prodigal's Return* that attracted most comment when it was first exhibited at the Royal Academy, London, in 1869 was the way in which the prodigal turned his head away from his wounded father. He is unable to look him in the eye. The father gazes tenderly on his son, perhaps finding it difficult to believe that his son has been restored to him. The son, however, cannot return his father's affection. He is ashamed, unable to believe that he has found the acceptance for which he yearned, yet which lay far beyond his right. As one critic wrote at the time, perhaps a little ponderously: 'So much shame and contrition, so many recollections of truest affection abused and betrayed, such remorseful gratitude for the un-upbraiding, unhesitating welcome which the father has hastened to give are expressed or suggested in that sidelong look that we feel further comment, apology, or illustration from our pen would be an impertinence.'

The parable helps us open up this opulent concept of redemption. We see immediately how the idea of restoration is of central importance. What was lost has been found. A precious relationship that was fractured and ruptured has been restored and renewed. Yet there is another insight here, nestling within these great themes, that is so easily overlooked. It is this: *the redeemed life is better than innocent existence.* Why?

To understand this point, we have to try to place ourselves in the son's position, and see things as he saw them. He was a privileged family member, enjoying the comfort and intimacy of his father's house. Yet he was discontented and restless. The grass was greener on the other side of the fence – or, in this case, in the distant country that seemed to offer him the fulfilment of his dreams. His future lay in that far land, not in the familiar, humdrum world that he knew so well. Somewhere, sometime, his dreams would come true.

But they didn't. Living in that foreign place gave him a sense of perspective that he could never have had while he remained at home. He was able to see his home situation from outside. And suddenly, it seemed much more attractive. The grass was not greener in those distant lands. The son's experience helped him realize that his original situation had been infinitely better. But this insight could only be gained by walking away from his home.

The son's recognition of the privileges and joys of home only came through bitter experience of its alternatives. In his innocent state, the son knew nothing else. He had nothing to compare his state with, and believed that others were better. From the vantage point of his exile, he realized the truth – but it was a truth that he could only learn from afar. Redemption was about returning home, with a new sense of appreciation of the benefits of his home, and the privilege of those who lived there. The reaction of the second, older son is important here. We cannot help but feel sympathy for him. He remained faithful. He did not need to leave home to know its joy or to know his father's love.

The son's return was not simply geographical; it was relational. He had not only a long physical journey to make, but also an even more difficult personal journey: he needed to change. He had to become in reality the son that he was at present only in name. He needed to be reconciled to his father – something which he knew he had no right to expect and yet which he longed for more than anything. Redemption is about coming home from our distant lands and becoming what God wants us to be.

Lord, help us to appreciate the privilege and wonder of being your children. Help us never to take them for granted.

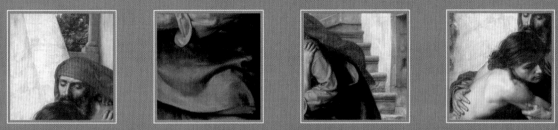

deliverance from bondage

Imagine that you are being asked to explain what 'reconciliation' means. You might offer a standard dictionary definition, and talk about 'addressing and resolving conflictual and fractured relationships'. This is better than nothing, but it is rather like seeing a distant mountain range through the mist: you know it's there, you know it's important, but you haven't quite managed to see it properly.

Instead, you might tell the story of how you were reconciled to a friend or family member. The story would involve explaining how your relationship broke down, leading into what happened to restore it, and the difference it makes. Suddenly, the mountain range comes into sharp focus; it is something that has become real and personal, something that matters, something with the capacity to change lives.

When Christians talk about redemption, they tell a story. As we saw in the previous chapter, it is a long, wonderful and many-sided story, which tells of 'the loving purposes of God from the first days of our disobedience unto the glorious Redemption brought us by this Holy Child,' retold throughout the Christian year, above all at Christmas and Easter.

For Israel, the greatest act of God's many acts of redemption was the deliverance of Israel from her bondage in Egypt. Moses was raised up by God to set his people free. Seeing that his people were oppressed and enslaved, God prepared the way for their deliverance and their eventual entry into the promised land of Canaan. The exodus brought Israel into existence as the people of God. It was their story, about their God. In retelling this story, Israel shaped her identity in the present and nourished her future hopes. It was a story that should never be forgotten.

So how could so great a story be remembered and passed on to future generations? How could Israel ensure that she never forgot those pivotal events of long, long ago? How could the memory of that great event and

its significance for Israel be kept alive? The answer lay in a ceremony – an act of recollection, to be undertaken every year, in which the exodus would be remembered, and the faithfulness and loving-kindness of God proclaimed and celebrated. The name of this act of remembrance? The Passover.

The basic shape of the Passover rite was simple, and laid down in the Old Testament itself.

> Observe the month of Abib by keeping the passover to the LORD your God, for in the month of Abib the LORD your God brought you out of Egypt by night. You shall offer the passover sacrifice to the LORD your God, from the flock and the herd, at the place that the LORD will choose as a dwelling for his name. You must not eat with it anything leavened. For seven days you shall eat unleavened bread with it – the bread of affliction – because you came out of the land of Egypt in great haste, so that all the days of your life you may remember the day of your departure from the land of Egypt. (Deuteronomy 16.1–4)

The central elements of the rite reminded Israel of her past – her bondage and oppression in Egypt and God's act of deliverance. The unleavened bread and the Passover lamb were symbols of that past.

As time passed, the Passover rite became more complex, but its central theme remained the same – remembering God's acts of deliverance and his promises to his people. A community's past is central to its identity. To destroy a people, all you need to do is break their link with the past, so that they have no memories – no sense of a shared history and no awareness of what binds them together and gives them their place in history.

The central symbols of the Passover were real, physical elements – lamb and bread, to which others, such as wine, were added in later times. These

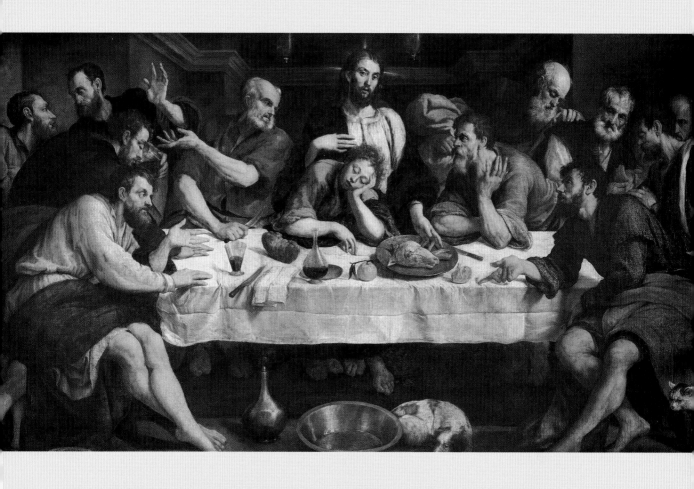

ordinary, physical objects became the focal point for this great act of recollection. Lamb and bread might be eaten regularly in other contexts. But on this one night of the year, they were charged with a deeper meaning. They became gateways of remembrance to an identity-giving past.

For Christians, it is of great importance that Jesus celebrated a Passover meal before being betrayed, handed over to the Roman authorities and led to execution. At the most basic of levels, it reminds us that Jesus and his disciples were Jews, who shared that community's memory of its past and hopes for its future, despite the humiliation of Israel at the hands of the Roman occupation force. Yet this barely touches the meaning of this event, traditionally known as the 'Last Supper'. As we reflect on its meaning, we shall allow our imaginations to be engaged and excited by an image of this Passover meal by Jacopo Bassano (1515–92).

Bassano's *Last Supper* is widely regarded as a masterpiece of sixteenth-century Italian art. It is not as familiar as Leonardo da Vinci's famous depiction of the same event, which is known to have inspired Bassano's work. Yet in its own way, Bassano's masterpiece is a far more powerful and insightful depiction of the scene. Whereas Leonardo's is carefully posed, the disciples symmetrically distributed around the table, Bassano conveys the spontaneity and disorder of the event. Stray cats and dogs have crept in to devour the scraps; the table cloth is crumpled and stained. Although Leonardo portrays the disciples as dressed in richly coloured robes, Bassano has them wearing their everyday garments, even emphasizing their bare feet. They look weary and exhausted, whereas Leonardo's disciples are alert and actively engaged in conversation.

It is clearly a Passover meal – notice the lamb's head, prominently displayed on the table, with bread to each side. A flagon of wine, an important part of the Passover celebration by this time in Israel's history, can also be seen. Yet Bassano displaces the bread, the wine and the lamb. None is central to his depiction of what is going on. The traditional symbols of the Passover are present, reaffirming God's presence and action in the past. Yet the central figure of the painting is Christ. It is as if Bassano is visually indicating his theological interpretation of the Last Supper – that whatever the Passover recalled and celebrated is somehow finding its fulfilment in Christ. The three symbols remain but they are now interpreted in a new way.

A fundamental theme of the Christian understanding of the significance of Jesus Christ is that he stands in continuity with Israel – yet brings a new people of God into being. He stands in continuity with the great saving acts of God in the past – but is himself the ground and agent of a greater act of redemption in the present. As Bassano hints, the symbols remain but now point to something – someone – else: someone greater than Moses is here.

First, let us consider the symbol of the lamb – a lamb that has clearly been slain, to judge by Bassano's representation. How are we to understand this? It is impossible for a biblically literate Christian to look at Bassano's *Last Supper* and avoid making a connection with some words of John the Baptist, as recorded in John's Gospel. When John sees Christ coming towards him, he declares: 'Here is the Lamb of God who takes away the sin of the world!' (John 1.29). The image of the lamb remains; it is now redirected, not simply towards the person of Jesus, but to an understanding of what he achieves: the taking away of the sin of the world. As the 'Lamb of God', Jesus is contiguous with the exodus, while also transcending it through a new act of redemption – the deliverance of humanity from sin.

Yet the image of the lamb prompts still further reflection. The prophecy of Isaiah speaks of a coming suffering servant, who would be like 'a lamb that is led to the slaughter' (Isaiah 53.7), on whom the guilt and sin of the world are laid. Perhaps John the Baptist had this rich vein of biblical prophecy in mind when he spoke of Christ as the 'the Lamb of God, *who takes away the sin of the world*'. This immediately suggests an affinity with the scapegoat (Leviticus 16.21–22), which was sent into the wilderness bearing the sin of God's people.

Yet the bread and the wine also undergo a radical change in significance. As the Passover meal that we know as the Last Supper proceeds, the bread and the wine are given a new meaning.

> Then [Jesus] took a loaf of bread, and when he had given thanks, he broke it and gave it to them, saying, 'This is my body, which is given for you. Do this in remembrance of me.' And he did the same with the cup after supper, saying, 'This cup that is poured out for you is the new covenant in my blood. But see, the one who betrays me is with me, and his hand is on the table'. (Luke 22.19–21)

These words have shaped both the Christian understanding of what Christ achieved, and how this is to be remembered and proclaimed. Without losing their associations with the exodus from Egypt, the bread and wine now become linked with the significance of Christ's forthcoming death.

So how is that death to be understood? We remember the event

itself; but should we not also remember its interpretation? Or be forced to rethink what it means each time we recall it? The Gospels record only one explicit statement of Jesus concerning the meaning of his death, which is all the more important for this reason. When some of his disciples were busy bickering, in an-all-too human manner, over which of them was the most important, Jesus silenced them with the following words:

> Whoever wishes to be first among you must be slave of all. For the Son of Man came not to be served but to serve, and to give his life a ransom for many. (Mark 10.44–45)

The image of Christ's death as a 'ransom' offers us a clue to the meaning of redemption, as well as clarifying his language about the bread and wine at the Last Supper.

So what is a ransom? The idea is as familiar to us today as it was in the time of Christ. The image invites us to use our imaginations to construct a scenario. Some people are in captivity. They are being held against their will and are unable to break free from their captivity. Unless someone is able to liberate them, they will remain trapped. So how might liberation come about? Through storming the prison, breaking down its gates, and allowing them to go free? This is the famous image of the 'harrowing of hell', beloved of medieval Christian writers. Yet there is another possibility – someone paying the ransom price that is demanded.

The implications of this possibility are enormous. Why should anyone want to liberate someone in this way, unless the person being held was very special or really mattered to someone? The greater the value of the individual, the greater the ransom demanded by the captors.

The Christian gospel is clear on this point: God showed his love for us by paying an astonishing, unsurpassable, ransom for each of us. The sense of amazement that this evokes can be seen in the poem by Richard Crashaw (1613–49) entitled 'Charitas Nimia; or, The Dear Bargain':

> Lord, what is man? why should he cost Thee
> So dear? what had his ruin lost Thee?
> Lord, what is man, that Thou hast over-bought
> So much a thing of naught?

For Crashaw, God had no need to redeem us. He could have continued to rule the world, indifferent to our hopeless situation.

> Alas, sweet Lord! what were't to Thee
> If there were no such worms as we?
> Heav'n ne'er the less still Heav'n would be,
> Should mankind dwell
> In the deep hell.
> What have his woes to do with Thee?

Yet God chose to act otherwise, demonstrating his love in our redemption. God could not ignore us, precisely because we matter so much to him.

By remembering the 'loving purposes of God from the first days of our disobedience unto the glorious Redemption brought us by this Holy Child', we are being reassured of the reality and unconditional nature of that love. While we were still sinners, Christ died for us. God loves us – and he shows that love by his actions, by doing something that both transforms our situation and demonstrates the full extent of his love for us. As we think about redemption, we must certainly reflect on what this rich word means. But we must also reflect on what it presupposes – our need for redemption in the first place, and the gracious love of God in providing it in the second.

Lord, help us to remember you. Help us to call to mind all that you have done for us. Help us to realize how precious we are to you. And help us also to reflect that love in the way we behave.

the battle within us

Year by year, as we retell the story of 'the loving purposes of God from the first days of our disobedience unto the glorious Redemption brought us by this Holy Child', we recall not only the redemption that God has achieved but also the tragedy of the human situation that led God to act in this way. To speak about redemption is implicitly to speak of our *need* for redemption. The world is not the way it is meant to be. We, too, are not the way we are meant to be. Something has gone wrong somewhere – something so serious that it cannot be put right on the basis of the resources that we ourselves can muster. All of our relationships seem to have gone wrong – our relationship with the earth, with each other and with God. What, we sometimes wonder, happened to the great vision of the garden of Eden (Genesis 2), when humanity walked with God in the cool of the day? Might God one day come back, to walk again with his people in such a garden?

In *The Taking of Christ*, Caravaggio (1571–1610) provides a powerful visual interpretation of how far things have gone astray from God's original intentions for humanity. When God did visit his people – a central theme of the Christian doctrine of the incarnation – he was betrayed, not welcomed, in a garden. A kiss, normally a sign of affection and commitment, became perverted into a sign of rejection and betrayal. Caravaggio focuses on this moment of betrayal, described in the Gospels: 'The one I will kiss is the man; arrest him' (Matthew 26.48). Christ's eyes are averted, turned down so that he cannot see the face of his betrayer. He knows who it is; he does not need to look. His hands are clasped together in a gesture of resignation. He must indeed drink the cup of suffering. It will not be taken away from him.

Caravaggio freezes the action of this chilling moment in the gospel narratives of the last week of Christ's life. At one level, the dark background conveys the fact that the betrayal and arrest took place at night. Yet at another, it suggests the theological notion of the darkness of the world

trying to extinguish the light that has come into its midst. The centrepiece is neither Christ nor his betrayer, but the soldier's outstretched, armour-encased arm, touching the face of Christ. It is not the gentle touch of one of his disciples but the cold, commanding gesture of a figure of authority. And where are the disciples? Caravaggio depicts Christ as alone, surrounded by his enemies. To the left, we see one of the disciples fleeing in terror, abandoning Christ to his fate.

Caravaggio's powerful representation of the betrayal of Christ in Gethsemane highlights the theological point that underlies the whole question of redemption. How far has this world fallen, when its religious and political leaders betray their God on his entry into his world! If this world were as God intended it to be, his visit would have been welcomed with delight and admiration. Christ's triumphal entry into Jerusalem might seem to suggest that all was well – God's people welcoming their Messiah into his city. Yet this response turns out to be superficial. Deeper, darker forces triumph over those good intentions. They prove irresistible. Humanity is unable to check its deepest desires, its most fundamental impulses. Those might once have been directed towards God. But not now. Something has gone wrong. And it is something that we are powerless to put right.

In the gospel accounts of the last days of Christ, Christ is betrayed by a kiss. Yet at a deeper level, he is betrayed by human nature itself. We are tempted to rush in to blame Judas Iscariot for this shameful act. We would never have done anything like that! Or we try to place the blame for the death of Christ on the Roman political authorities or the Jewish religious leaders. The New Testament will have none of this. This attempt to shift the blame to scapegoats will not do. The deeply unsettling thought that we must take away from that gospel scene is that we might have done the same. We, who like to think we are the solution to the world's ills, are actually part of

the problem. Caravaggio's scene is about the failings of human nature and our need for redemption. We need to be saved from ourselves.

It is a deeply disturbing idea, which makes us highly uncomfortable. We want to believe that we would do the right things. Like Peter, we want to believe that we would do anything for Christ. Yet as Peter discovered to his horror, 'The spirit indeed is willing, but the flesh is weak' (Matthew 26.41). Why is it that we fail to live up to our own aspirations? In a letter to his publisher Atticus, the great Roman orator Marcus Tullius Cicero commented that he wished that he did not have to grow old and see all the hopes and dreams of his youth crumble and collapse in the face of the realities of human nature.

It is a serious issue that has provoked much debate within Christianity. Perhaps the most famous of these debates took place between Pelagius and Augustine in the closing years of the Roman empire. For Pelagius, God created human nature fundamentally good, and it remained so. When God commanded us to do good and avoid evil, he expected us to be able to do them. After all, God made us, and must know what we are capable of doing. Living up to God's expectations is thus about pulling ourselves together, keeping the commandments and imitating Christ.

This can-do, brash confidence in human nature is echoed down the centuries, finding expression in the celebrated poem 'Invictus' by William Ernest Henley (1849–1903), which proclaims our mastery of our condition:

> I am the master of my fate;
> I am the captain of my soul!

Augustine believed that this entire outlook rested on a hopelessly unrealistic conception of human nature. Yes, God created humanity good. But something had gone wrong. Had not Paul himself reflected on the fatal tensions within human nature, which undermined Pelagius' confidence in human ability?

> For I know that nothing good dwells within me, that is, in my flesh. I can will what is right, but I cannot do it. For I do not do the good I want, but the evil I do not want is what I do. Now if I do what I do not want, it is no longer I that do it, but sin that dwells within me. So I find it to be a law that when I want to do what is good, evil lies close at hand. (Romans 7.18–21)

So what can be done? For Paul, the answer sums up much of the Christian understanding of the relationship of God and humanity – redemption in Christ:

> Wretched man that I am! Who will rescue me from this body of death? Thanks be to God through Jesus Christ our Lord! (Romans 7.24–25)

It is this Pauline understanding of the human predicament and its solution that Augustine explores. For Augustine, we are trapped in our own situation. He develops image after image to illuminate our predicament. We are in darkness, and cannot see. We are ill, and cannot heal ourselves. We are injured, and need someone to bind our wounds. We are trapped, and cannot break free from our captivity. We are addicted to patterns of behaviour that we cannot master. We need an illuminator, a healer, a liberator. Augustine argues that God's graciousness is demonstrated through providing what fallen human nature requires. Redemption is about engaging human nature at its many points of need so that it may be transformed and renewed.

Augustine's account of human nature is sometimes criticized as being unduly pessimistic. His response would be to argue that he is merely being realistic, confronting the difficult, painful questions of real human existence that he believed Pelagius ignored. Pelagius, by inflating expectations of what humanity could achieve, was living in an unreal world, unwilling to confront the darker side of human nature.

Christian writers down the ages, of all theological persuasions, have stressed the consequence of the 'double knowledge of God': in other words, knowing the truth about God and about ourselves. We must learn to see ourselves as we really are, rather than accept the rather flattering self-images that we construct or allow others to create for us. Reflecting on the betrayal of Christ is disturbing and uncomfortable precisely because it challenges us to see ourselves through the lens of that event and to see the struggles taking place within our own souls.

John Donne's poem 'Hymn to God, my God, in my sickness' explores this inner tension within the dynamics of the Christian life by reflecting on the Pauline image of Christ as the second Adam:

We think that Paradise and Calvary,
Christ's cross and Adam's tree, stood in one place;
Look, Lord, and find both Adams met in me;
As the first Adam's sweat surrounds my face,
May the last Adam's blood my soul embrace.

Donne here draws on an approach developed by the second-century writer Irenaeus of Lyons, one of the Church's greatest theologians. In the story of Jesus Christ, Irenaeus discerned a pattern of redemption which seemed to retrace the wayward steps of humanity, correcting its errors and setting it back on the right track. Using the Pauline image of 'recapitulation' in a way that might have surprised Paul, Irenaeus argued that Christ went over the main points (hence 'recapitulation') of Adam's sorry history, embracing and transforming it. Adam's disobedience took place in a garden and forfeited eternal life; Christ's obedience took place in a garden and regained eternal life. For Adam, the tree of life became a tree of death; in Christ, the tree of death became a tree of life. And so on. This is not really a rigorous theological analysis, more a noting of patterns and the improvisation of a theological analogy that weaves them together into a more or less coherent pattern. But the theme is fundamental to Christian theology: 'For just as by the one man's disobedience the many were made sinners, so by the one man's obedience the many will be made righteous' (Romans 5.19).

Whereas Irenaeus surveys the coincidences of themes, events and locations in the historical actualization of salvation, Donne invites us to turn away from this bold panorama of history and to see the great themes of redemption transferred to a smaller stage – our own lives. His imagery depicts the tension, even the struggle, in the lives of Christians between the lingering power and presence of sin and the transforming power of divine grace.

Donne transfers the struggle that Irenaeus locates in salvation history to the interior world of each individual. At one level, the struggle is between two different mindsets, two ways of thinking. The natural order demands that we think in terms of redemption by 'sweat': a reference to the work that Adam was commanded to undertake after the Fall. Salvation, within this mindset, is the result of our achievements – something that we ourselves do. Donne wants us to contrast this with a Christian mindset, which thinks of redemption being based, not upon what we do, but upon what has been done for us – namely, Christ's work on the cross. The tension between 'Adam's sweat' and 'Christ's blood' is between the law of works and the way of grace. Part of the discipleship of the mind we are called to as Christians is to reorient our hopes, expectations and prayer to fit in with this grace-filled and grace-directed way of thinking and living.

But Donne's words point us to another, even more important, level of conflict. There is a battle taking place within us, between the old Adam and the new, between our old selves and our new selves (Ephesians 4.22–24). The emblems of each identity – Adam's tree and Christ's cross – remain.

Whatever else the Christian life may, be it is about the triumph of the latter over the former. We cannot totally break free from the limits of our humanity. Yet Christ's death and resurrection inaugurate something new within our lives that will ultimately unseat our former master, undo our bonds to our past ways of living and thinking, and unleash the full power of God's grace to heal and to transform. Although we are loved by God and have been accepted by God, sin abides within us. Martin Luther once argued that the Christian is *simul iustus et peccator* – at one and the same time a righteous person and a sinner.

God loves sinners – we must never lose sight of that insight. We do not need to be perfect to be loved by God. Yet that gracious acceptance leads to personal transformation. No one who knows God's love is left unchanged by it.

Lord, help us to confront our old natures – the 'old Adam' that lingers within all of us. May your grace transform and renew us.

being judged

being judged

Some of the most dramatic moments in Jesus Christ's final week in Jerusalem highlight the theme of judgement. Christ is brought before the religious, and then the secular, authorities of his day, who cast judgement on him. Christian writers have often paused here, taking time to reflect on the implications of these events. The paradox was obvious. God had entered his world – the world that he had created – and was rejected by it. 'He was in the world, and the world came into being through him; yet the world did not know him. He came to what was his own, and his own people did not accept him' (John 1. 10–11). The judge of all was judged by others and found guilty.

The gospel accounts betray no hostility towards either the Jewish or Roman leaders as they relate how Jesus was brought before both, to face condemnation and death. Both Jew and Roman are seen as representing fallen humanity in general, whether in its religious or political forms. There is no place in Christianity for scapegoating any individuals or groups for the death of Christ. The gospel accounts of the double trial of Jesus before Caiaphas and Pilate simply do not permit us to make the cheap and easy judgement that someone else was responsible. The problem lay not with Caiaphas nor Pilate, nor with Jew or Roman in the first century. The Christian Church has always insisted, and rightly, that the ultimate cause of Christ's Passion and death was flawed and fallen human nature – something in which we all share, and something that we all represent and embody. It is not a particularly pleasant or reassuring thought. We, it turns out, are the ones who are being judged.

The trial of Christ before Pontius Pilate is seen as being of especial importance. It is no accident that the name of this minor Roman official has found its way into the Christian creeds. When Christians affirm that 'Christ suffered under Pontius Pilate', they are pointing to a critical moment in the intertwined stories of God and humanity. Pilate is not being blamed for

Christ's death; that death is simply being located at a specific moment in the reality of human history. The incarnation was, it reminds us, about God entering into a tiny slice of human history with the capacity to illuminate and transform that history as a whole.

So what do we know of the historical figure of Pontius Pilate? Not that much, really. All that remains of his achievements as a Roman official is a single limestone block found amidst the ruins of Caesarea, bearing a fragmentary inscription with his name and office: PONTIVS PILATVS PRAEFECTVS IVDAEAE. There are good reasons for suggesting that he may have been relatively young and inexperienced. However, even his critics allow that he managed to keep the peace in that region for ten years during a particularly difficult and turbulent period. His name associates him with the Pontius family. This immediately suggests that he was not a patrician, a member of the Roman nobility. The Pontii were not pure Romans, but Samnites – the Italian tribesmen conquered by the Romans in the third century BC. Pilate would never secure the high public office in Rome that was reserved for the Roman nobility.

The trial of Jesus before Pilate is perhaps best envisaged through the superb painting *Ecce Homo* by the Swiss-born Italian artist Antonio Ciseri (1821–91). This striking painting conveys a remarkable sense of place and allows us to make some important theological comments on the trial of Christ. The title *Ecce Homo* ('Behold, the man!') is derived from the account of Christ's trial provided in John's Gospel, although Ciseri incorporates elements from other gospel accounts of this event. The painting allows us to reflect on the central section of John's account of the trial (John 18.37–38).

Pilate asked him, 'So you are a king?' Jesus answered, 'You say that I am a king. For this I was born, and for this I came into the world, to

testify to the truth. Everyone who belongs to the truth listens to my voice.' Pilate asked him, 'What is truth?' After he had said this, he went out to the Jews again and told them, 'I find no case against him.'

Having made this statement, Pilate asks the crowd who they want released, following a Passover custom. The crowd demands the release of Barabbas.

Ciseri freezes the scene at the point at which Pilate, having asked Jesus whether he is indeed a king, turns away to face the crowd. The scene is brilliantly, even sumptuously, depicted. Pilate stands at the centre, the focus of attention. He is surrounded by symbols of personal and institutional power. Our eyes take in the Roman triumphal column immediately to Pilate's right, the throne behind him, and the soldiers guarding Christ, one of whom is holding another symbol of power: the legionary standard. Ahead of Pilate, an immense crowd throngs the streets. Some have even climbed onto nearby buildings to observe what is going on. The scene exudes conflict and tension – the power of the crowd, the power of the Roman state, and the seemingly powerless, helpless and hopeless figure of Jesus of Nazareth, whose attitude seems to indicate resignation. He has submitted himself to what is to come.

Christ has spoken of truth; Pilate responds with an offhand, seemingly cynical comment: 'What is truth?' It is a scene often associated with one of the best-known sayings of Francis Bacon (1561–1626): 'What is truth?, said jesting Pilate; and would not stay for an answer'. What did Pilate mean by this? For some, it is the cynical comment of a politician. Pilate's world is not one in which truth features prominently. He seeks approval, not truth.

And it was not a judgement that all found acceptable. To the right, we see Pilate's wife. Her face is resolutely turned away from her husband, as she leans on another woman for support. We do not even know the name of Pilate's wife, although tradition has it that she was Claudia Procula (or perhaps 'Procla'). In another gospel account of these proceedings, we learn that she was convinced of Jesus' innocence (Matthew 27.19). Her head is downcast, her eyes closed. Every aspect of her body language indicates distress.

Ciseri captures the dark mood of the moment perfectly. Note how Pilate, having asked what truth might be, *turns away* from the one who not only can answer that question, but is himself its answer. He turns away from the one who *is* the truth to those who, for his purposes that afternoon, shall determine what truth shall be. Truth is what people want it to be. See how Pilate's head is bowed towards the crowd. He will submit to whatever it takes for him to keep the peace and, thus, to keep his job.

The judgement that Pilate offers is that of a world-weary politician, driven by expediency and compromise. A wrong judgement on his part, and he would have a riot on his hands. We shall never know how many situations like this he had encountered before. But he is remembered only for this one deeply cynical judgement. Yet it is an instinct that is deeply built into our culture. We believe what we want to believe. We construct our own realities and wish to be judged by them.

Judgement is a word that many find deeply threatening. It implies evaluation, accountability and the possibility of being found wanting. It is something that many of us try to avoid. We prefer to judge ourselves and often find our own verdicts entirely to our own liking. As Christian spiritual writers down the ages have pointed out, the essence of sin is self-deception: a refusal to face up to the way things actually are; an evasion of awkward realities, when convenient half-truths lie to hand; the manipulative use of language to disguise evil as good.

But perhaps more importantly, judgement implies that authority lies beyond us. We prefer to judge others, and thus to stand over them. To concede that we might stand under someone is an alarming thought to those who crave autonomy. We cannot bear to hear words of judgement or to step into the light, for fear it will show us up for what we really are. 'This is the judgement, that the light has come into the world, and people loved darkness rather than light' (John 3.19).

It is a theme that is often found in the works of the great Russian novelist Fyodor Dostoevsky (1821–81). Commentators have often noted Dostoevsky's perceptive analysis of human nature and its tensions. Humanity appears in Dostoevsky's works as a tragic, split creature, excluded from paradise but longing for reconciliation. Nicholas Berdyaev suggested that Dostoevsky 'uncovered a volcanic crater in every being'. This is especially clear in *The Devils* (also known as *The Possessed*), the third of Dostoevsky's five great novels. The work describes the activities of a revolutionary group seeking to overthrow the Russian government and weaken the influence of the Church. This conspiracy demands absolute secrecy on the part of the group's members, as they prepare to commit a series of horrific crimes in pursuit of their political goal. In Dostoevsky's hands, this becomes a penetrating criticism of absolute human autonomy and a shrewd evaluation of the implications of atheism for human nature.

One of the novel's chief characters is an intellectual, Kirillov, who argues that the non-existence of God legitimates all forms of actions. Kirillov rejects belief in God. So what remains? If there is no God, he argues, it follows that he, Kirillov, is God:

> If God exists, then everything is His will, and I can do nothing of my own apart from His will. If there's no God, then everything is my will, and I'm bound to express my self-will.

Since the idea of God is a pure human invention, Kirillov reasons that he is free to do as he pleases. There is no divine judgement to fear. He is the one who makes the rules.

So what has this idea of judgement to do with our theme of redemption? Among the many things that might be noted here, perhaps one point stands out – the need for honesty. The gospel challenges two unacceptable views of human nature: the proud, hopelessly optimistic account that sees humanity as self-sufficient, capable of perfecting itself and securing its own salvation; and the pessimistic, defeatist view that insists human nature is worthless, hopeless and insignificant. It is only when we see ourselves as we really are that we realize our need for transformation and our own inability to bring this about. The Christian gospel beautifully marries divine affirmation with divine judgement. In reflecting on the cross of Christ, we realize both the extent of God's love for us, and our need for redemption.

So what is our problem? And how does the gospel connect up with our predicament and transform it? The great tradition of Christian theology has reflected long and hard on this matter, nourished by Scripture and Christian experience. Among the images that have been found to be illuminating, we may note the following. We are lost; Christ has come to find us. We are ill; Christ has come to bind our wounds. We cannot see; Christ has come to illuminate our minds and the path ahead of us. We are alone; Christ has come to accompany us and guide us, as our shepherd. We are guilty; Christ has come to purge that guilt and renew us morally. We are held captive by sin and our mortality; Christ has come to break their power and set us free.

We naturally think of judgement in a legal context, as, for example, condemnation. Yet it is helpful to think of it medically. When a doctor diagnoses an illness, she is passing a judgement on her patient, telling him what is wrong with him – but doing so in order that the patient may be cured. Diagnosis must never be confused with condemnation. If we are told that we are seriously ill, we condemn ourselves if we refuse to act on the basis of our knowledge of what is wrong on the one hand, and how that situation may be remedied on the other. *In order to be cured, we need to know what is wrong with us.* The first step in the process of healing is identifying what the problem is.

For the Christian, judgement is not God's humiliation of humanity or a degradation of human nature. It is God's request that we see ourselves as we really are and face up to that reality. Accepting this judgement may involve swallowing our pride and hearing some very uncomfortable realities. But facing up to the way things are is always the prelude to transformation.

Lord, help us to hear your words of judgement, that we may know the truth about ourselves and be set free from bondage to our old natures.

the death of Christ

Christian spirituality stresses the importance of an imaginative encounter with the crucified Christ in order to avoid abstract, impersonal, dehistoricized ways of thinking about the theological significance of this event. It is fatally easy to marginalize the actual historical events of Good Friday and concentrate on 'theories of the atonement' – in other words, ideas about what those events mean. Yet we impoverish the meaning of the cross if we try to reduce it to ideas, or think of forgiveness as some kind of commercial or legal transaction. Still worse, we may drive a wedge between the real historical event of Christ's Passion and death and the benefits that this brings, as if we can speak of the latter independently of the means by which they are achieved.

We must come to terms with Christ as he was on the cross – battered, bruised, bleeding and betrayed. Our minds must take in what our imaginations, nourished by the biblical Passion narratives, set before them. C. S. Lewis's enigmatic remark is helpful here: 'While reason is the natural organ of truth, imagination is the organ of meaning.'

One of the most important Christian spiritual writers is Ignatius Loyola (1491–1556). Formerly a soldier, Loyola appreciated the importance of discipline in the spiritual life. In his *Spiritual Exercises*, he set out a programme of engagement with the life of Christ and the basics of the Christian faith that made a powerful appeal to the imagination. We are to read the New Testament from the standpoint of active participation. And how are we to do this? By projecting ourselves into the gospel narratives, and seeing the events they describe as taking place before our eyes and in our presence. We are to join the disciples as they see, hear and reflect,

deepening their understanding and appreciation of who Christ is and what he has done.

At no point is this approach more effective than engaging with the crucifixion. Loyola will not allow us to theorize about the crucifixion, substituting theological analysis for personal commitment and spiritual transformation. He asks his readers to enter into a dialogue with the dying Christ over the costliness of the redemption that will come about through his death, and the love of the creator in redeeming the fallen and broken creation. In his *Spiritual Exercises*, Loyola invites his readers to imagine themselves as being present at Calvary. He asks them to set aside any misgivings they may have about what he proposes and to engage in a dialogue with the dying Christ. Initially this involves reflection on what is happening: the creator suffering for the creation, the one who has eternal life by right choosing to suffer physical pain and death for sinners. Then this meditation is used as a means for self-examination, with a view for setting a future agenda for spiritual growth and discipline.

Imagine Christ our Lord before you, hanging upon the cross.
Talk to him about how the creator became a human being, and how he who possesses eternal life submitted himself to physical death for our sins. Then I shall reflect on myself, and ask:

What have I done for Christ?
What am I now doing for Christ?
What ought I to do for Christ?

As I see him like this, hanging upon the cross, I shall meditate on what comes to mind.

Many feel uneasy about this notion of talking to Christ in this way, feeling that it is inappropriate and possibly distasteful. Yet it is a hesitation that may be overcome to considerable advantage. The dialogue which Loyola wishes those undertaking the Exercises to enter into has the effect of moving them from thought to action. After reflecting on what Christ has done for us, Loyola demands that we ask what we are doing for Christ. And that answer is likely to be embarrassing on account of its inadequacy.

So how can we catalyse this process of imaginative engagement with the cross? The simplest answer is also the most effective: by allowing an image to stimulate our thoughts. In what follows, we shall use one of the twentieth century's most striking representations of the crucifixion to stimulate our imaginations. *Christ of St John of the Cross* (1951) is a late, and by far the most popular, work of the Spanish artist Salvador Dalí (1904–89). The work arrests our attention through its unusual perspective on Christ, its bold colours, extraordinary lighting, and intriguing surface effects. Although the look of the work was regarded as something of a cheap gimmick by most critics, it has gone on to secure acceptance and popular acclaim as a theologically astute representation of the crucifixion.

Most find their attention drawn immediately to the figure of Christ himself. As we explore the picture, however, we shall begin from the bottom and work upwards. The lower scene depicts two fishermen, standing by the shore of a preternaturally brilliant and gorgeous lake. Immediately, we identify it as the Sea of Galilee. Is this Dalí's way of reminding us of the calling of the first disciples? On closer inspection, things turn out to be a little more complex. The fishermen are wearing seventeenth-century dress.

the death of Christ

In fact, they seem to have been copied from Diego Velázquez's *The Surrender of Breda*, painted some time before 1635. And the 'lake' is actually a harbour – in this case, Dalí's home town of Port Lligat, on the Spanish Costa Brava, which had already featured in his *The Madonna of Port Lligat* (1950).

Then we realize what is going on. Dalí, like other leading Spanish artists of the twentieth century, including Picasso, regarded Velázquez as Spain's greatest painter. Port Lligat is the place where Dalí lived. What Dalí has done is to recast the calling of the disciples, setting it in the cultural, intellectual and geographical world that he knew so well. The calling has been transposed to the realities of Dalí's own world of everyday life and artistic aspiration.

Our eyes then begin to rise, as we take in the figure of Christ. Where most conventional portrayals of the crucifixion set the viewer beneath the cross, forcing them to look upwards, Dalí sets us above the cross, inducing a sense of vertigo. The scenario appears to be a physical impossibility – the crucified Christ, suspended in mid-air. This astonishing perspective, according to Dalí, was based on a drawing attributed to the great Spanish mystical writer St John of the Cross (1542–91), now in the Monastery of the Incarnation at Ávila. The Christ of St John of the Cross hangs without any obvious support, his head down and arms stretched tight, as if he is straining to break free from the wooden frame enclosing him.

For Dalí, the cross seemed to be presented to the viewer as if it were a crucifix being held towards someone who is dying, so that they might behold and kiss their Saviour. To enter into Dalí's vision for this painting, try to imagine that you are lying on your deathbed with an unseen hand holding the cross above you. You cannot see anything other than the cross itself. You can only focus on it and reflect on what you see. It is an ideal stimulus to the spiritual reflections that Ignatius Loyola believed would reinvigorate the

Christian life. The anticipation of death is a powerful incentive to live the life of faith to the full.

And what is the relation between the two parts of the painting? Dalí offers us few hints. He tells us of a dream in the year 1950, in which he saw the metaphysical unity of all things being sustained by Christ. This is a theme found in many patristic writers, who saw redemption as a cosmic event. An anonymous fourth-century writer, 'Pseudo-Hippolytus', wrote of the cosmic dimensions of the cross as holding together the various aspects of reality on earth and in heaven. Does some such vision underlie Dalí's representation?

Perhaps. Yet as I have reflected on this painting, often using it for devotional purposes, I have found another explanation more compelling. Suppose we take Dalí at his word, and we think of the work as suggesting a crucifix held out to a dying person, reassuring them of the love of their Saviour for them, and of the reality of the salvation that he has won for them. Where he has gone, they too will follow. Now they say that, when dying, some see the most significant moments of their lives flash past them in an instant. Might this be a clue to what Dalí has in mind? Is not the first meeting of a believer with Christ, by their own equivalent of the shores of Lake Galilee, one of the most significant things ever to have happened? And might the surreal colours of the lakeside scene be a means of hinting at the

subtle effects of memory, as a life-changing moment is recalled, yet tinged with the roseate hues of nostalgia? It is a theme hinted at in Dalí's *The Persistence of Memory* (1931). If so, the *Christ of St John of the Cross* can be seen as integrating memory and hope in the face of death, a powerful reminder of some fundamental gospel themes.

Yet however we choose to interpret this painting, it remains a powerful depiction of the death of Christ on the cross, capable of sustaining our imaginative interplay with Christ, as Ignatius Loyola requests. So let us undertake this spiritual exercise, allowing Dalí to unlock our imaginations.

Loyola asks us to reflect on the mystery of the incarnation, which led Christ to the cross. So let us try to visualize the scene at Calvary. Perhaps you might read one of the gospel Passion narratives to help set the scene, taking the text slowly, and trying to allow yourself time to build up a mental picture of what is happening. You might find some of the illustrations used in earlier chapters helpful. But concentrate now on the cross, using Dalí to help you contemplate its meaning. You may find his unusual perspective helpful as you try to imagine the scene. This section from Mark's Passion narrative is particularly important at this point.

Those who passed by derided him, shaking their heads and saying,
'Aha! You who would destroy the temple and build it in three
days, save yourself, and come down from the cross!' In the same
way the chief priests, along with the scribes, were also mocking
him among themselves and saying, 'He saved others; he cannot save
himself. Let the Messiah, the King of Israel, come down from the cross
now, so that we may see and believe.' Those who were crucified with
him also taunted him. (Mark 15.29–32)

Here is the point: the crowds called upon Christ to come down from the
cross, and save himself. But he chose not to. He stayed there, and saved us
instead. He gave his utmost for us. That is what the love of God is like.

Something of Loyola's thoughts can be found in the writings of Richard
Crashaw (1613–49). In his 'Hymn of the Nativity', Crashaw celebrates the joy
of the birth of Christ:

Welcome all wonders in one sight!
Eternity shut in a span!
Summer in winter! day in night!
Heaven in earth! and God in man!
Great little one, whose all-embracing birth
Lifts earth to Heaven, stoops Heaven to earth!

But what of Christ's cross? In his 'Divine Epigrams', Crashaw frequently
reflects on the meaning of the cross for wounded, broken people such as
himself. Here, we find him reflecting on how Christ's wounds heal his:

Whatever story of their cruelty,
Or nail, or thorn, or spear have writ in Thee,
Are in another sense
 Still legible;
Sweet is the difference:
Once I did spell
Every red letter
A wound of Thine;
Now, what is better,
Balsam for mine.

Now, having brought both the believing mind and the believing imagination into play, as we reflect on the crucified Christ, let us hear those three questions once more:

What have I done for Christ?
What am I now doing for Christ?
What ought I to do for Christ?

I cannot answer those questions for you, nor you for me. But I know that they are profoundly uncomfortable questions, which cannot help but leave us unsettled. Yet in that unsettling, the wise find an opening for reflection and self-criticism – and hence growth and development.

Lord, help us to meditate on your sufferings on the cross, and the difference that your cross makes to our life and our thinking. May what we do for you reflect and be inspired by what you have done for us.

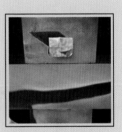

where was God?

After three hours of agony on the cross, Christ died. It is so easy, so very easy, for us to smile knowingly to ourselves. We know what happens next! The situation will soon be transformed! Or, to use the wonderful term invented by J. R. R. Tolkien, there will be a *eucatastrophe*, a moment of joy at deliverance from evil just at the point when all seemed to be lost. For Tolkien, the peculiar quality of the 'joy' in question concerns more than a sudden, unexpected turn of events; it is about 'a sudden glimpse of the underlying reality or truth' that moves readers to tears of joy.

But the tears shed at the end of the world's first Good Friday were not tears of joy. Forgotten were any promises of triumph, of resurrection. The disciples were confronted with the harsh, bitter reality of the death of Jesus of Nazareth. If we are ever to appreciate the experiential transfiguration of the totality of life that the resurrection enabled and disclosed, we must think ourselves into the situation of those first disciples, as that long day came to its end. An act of empathetic imagination is required of us by which we set aside the joy of resurrection and enter into the pure bleakness of Christ's death.

Perhaps the disciples had expected squadrons of angels to deliver their Lord from his instrument of execution. Perhaps they harboured hopes that, at the end of the day, he might detach himself from that cross and rejoin them, so that they might walk off together into the sunset, the past week's traumatic events left safely behind them. None of this happened. Christ died that same afternoon. And if we are to appreciate the *eucatastrophe* of the resurrection, we must first enter into the catastrophic experience of Christ's followers that afternoon.

Many Christian writers have tried to recreate the experience of that afternoon by standing with the disciples as they watched that desolate and demoralizing scene. The most famous of all is the poem 'Stabat Mater

dolorosa' by Jacopone da Todi (1230–1306), which allows the reader to share in Mary's sorrow at the death of her son. Da Todi seems to have regarded his poem as an extended meditation on the prophecy of Simeon that a sword was to pierce the heart of Jesus' mother, Mary (Luke 2.35), which is seen to be fulfilled in the crucifixion. Although this poem is best known in the translation of Edward Caswall (1814–78), what follows here is my literal translation of parts of the Latin text.

> The grieving Mother stood
> beside the cross, weeping,
> where her Son was hanging.
>
> Through her weeping soul,
> compassionate and grieving,
> a sword passed.
>
> For the sins of his people
> she saw Jesus in torment
> and subjected to the scourge.
>
> She saw her sweet Son
> dying, forsaken,
> while he gave up his spirit.

Christians have often found this deep sense of melancholy and bewilderment to be evoked more powerfully by images than by words. One of the most famous representations of the grief of Mary over the death of Christ was unveiled in St Peter's Basilica, Rome, in 1500. Michelangelo's *Pietà* is

regarded by many as one of the finest pieces of sculpture ever executed. Michelangelo was still only in his twenties when he created this masterpiece, which reworks the traditional imagery of Madonna and Child to convey the piteous grief of a mother over the death of her son. Mary holds the broken, still body of Christ in her arms, his face turned towards her.

The same scene is portrayed by El Greco (Domenikos Theotokopoulos, 1541–1614), the great Cretan artist who settled in Spain, where he produced some of his greatest masterpieces. His *Pietà* (c. 1572) seems to be closely modelled on a later version of this sculpture, created by Michelangelo in Florence in 1550, apparently intended to adorn his own tomb. This time, Michelangelo portrayed Mary holding Christ, attended by Joseph of Arimathea and Mary Magdalene. Following this pattern, El Greco pictures the scene, using a rich colouring technique he probably developed while working in Titian's Venice workshops in the late 1560s.

As El Greco depicts it, the scene is saturated with symbols of abandonment, desolation, rejection and humiliation. The group is seated at the foot of the cross, alone. The Twelve are nowhere to be seen. The crown of thorns lies to one side. Joseph of Arimathea stands by, ready to lend the desolate Christ a tomb to prevent his suffering the ultimate indignity of a pauper's common burial. On the other side, his hand is held by Mary Magdalene, whom the Gospels persistently identify as a witness to his teachings, healings and crucifixion. Following the tradition of the Church at this time, El Greco portrays her as a prostitute (note the dyed hair), although the Gospels themselves never explicitly make any such statement about her. It was common in much medieval devotional thought to distinguish between two Marys: one virtuous, the other fallen. Both are brought together here, in a powerful depiction of the levelling effect and social inclusiveness of the gospel.

So where is God in all this? There is no sign of his presence in this scene. In fact, the gospel accounts of the crucifixion and burial of Christ are saturated with the sense of the absence of God. Even the dying Christ seems to share that sense of abandonment. 'My God, my God, why have you forsaken me?' There was no divine intervention. No sign of divine presence, activity, compassion or existence. The first Good Friday is a narrative of the absence of God. Here is the 'dark night of the soul', so familiar to readers of St John of the Cross, when faith seems suspended without support from reason or experience.

Of course, we cannot tell the story of Good Friday without anticipating the radical inversion of affairs brought by the events of Easter Day. Yet to grasp the joy of that transformation, we must first enter into the bleak experience of that first Good Friday, experiencing it as pure cross, not as cross-leading-to-resurrection. We must share that sense of despair, hopelessness and helplessness that led those first disciples to abandon their Lord, as they seem to have believed him abandoned by his Lord.

One of the most astute guides to the spiritual relevance of this eerie feeling of utter hopelessness and helplessness is Martin Luther (1483–1546), himself no stranger to doubt and despair. Luther insists that the cross of Christ is the ultimate ground and judge of our thinking about God. The cross puts everything to the test. Luther argues that the picture of God so powerfully given to us by the cross is that of a deserted, bruised, bleeding and dying God, who lent new meaning and dignity to human suffering by passing through its shadow himself. God enters the world at the very point at which humanity is weak rather than strong, put to shame rather than proud. The darker and inevitable moments of life, culminating in pain, the knowledge of dying and death, are not areas of life from which God has been excluded, but areas in which he has deliberately chosen to be present.

This idea of the presence of God in the dark side of faith and life is given superb expression in Luther's famous statement: 'Abraham closed his eyes and hid himself in the darkness of faith – and found eternal light in its midst.' The powerful image of a God who knows what human suffering and pain are like, who *understands* at first hand what it is like to be weak, frail and mortal, is, Luther insists, authorized by the cross of Jesus Christ.

According to Luther, we should apply such insights to our own situation. There are times when all of us find it difficult to accept that God is present and active in the world – suffering being a case in point. If we try to think of these hard times in the light of Good Friday, we can see that those same thoughts and fears were expressed then. Yet the resurrection overturned those thoughts and fears, showing us how unreliable human experience is in these matters. Our present experience seems like Good Friday. God may not seem to be obviously present and active. But just as faith sees Good Friday from the standpoint of Easter Day, so it must also see the same patterns of interpretation in present experience. What looks like divine absence is really hidden divine presence.

Faith is thus an ability to see God's presence and activity in the world, and in our own experience. Faith sees behind external appearances and the misleading impressions of experience. It is an openness, a willingness, to

find God where he has promised to be, even when experience suggests that he is not there. This is what Luther means when he speaks of 'the darkness of faith'. God was indeed there on Good Friday, for those who had eyes to see him. That is the decisive verdict, delivered from the standpoint of Easter Day. The resurrection sets the crucifixion in perspective.

Yet Luther argues that our life in, and experience of, the world is often more like that first Good Friday. We are surrounded by pain, suffering and apparent divine abandonment, with no obvious sign of the presence of God. To use Luther's tantalizing phrase, we are dealing with a 'hidden God'. In this situation, Luther argues, we must hold fast to God in the darkness, trusting him even when our senses and experience seem to offer no grounds for such trust. We trust in God because of Christ, whose cross is both the foundation and criterion of our knowledge of him. Christian serenity is not about being spared from the storm, but knowing peace within that storm.

Similar ideas are explored by one of the finest Christian poets of the twentieth century. Although R. S. Thomas (1913–2000) was Welsh, he chose to write in English, thus making his ideas accessible to a much wider readership. Many of Thomas's poems celebrate the wild countryside of his native land, which he knew well from many years' experience as a rural priest. Yet others explore the themes of the Christian faith, especially the haunting theme of the seeming absence of God from his world. For many, Thomas is the 'poet of the hidden God', frequently evoking the image of an empty country church as a symbol of the deeper sense of the absence of God from our experiences of life.

Thomas's poem 'In a Country Church' asks us to imagine the poet kneeling before the God he believes to be there, yet hearing only the sound of the wind, and the whisper of the wings of bats, rather than angels. Thomas is a particularly severe critic of those who believe they can enclose or capture the elusive divine presence in institutions or buildings. His 'Empty Church' speaks of the futility of such aspirations. We may have created a stone trap for God, hoping to lure him there with candles, as though he would come like 'some huge moth, out of the darkness to beat there'. But instead, all that we find is silence. God does not speak.

One of Thomas's most moving poems is entitled 'Pietà'. This short poem takes the form of a reflection on the empty cross, Christ now resting in the arms of his mother. It is here that we find those questions about the presence of God being focused with such power and force. If this dead man was God incarnate, why is he now lying dead in his mother's arms? If this is how God treats his own son, how will he behave towards the rest of us? These are questions that lurk not far beneath the surface of our piety. We often suppress them for the sake of theological decency, hoping that they will go away. But they don't. And maybe they aren't meant to. Maybe it is by asking these hard, seemingly unanswerable questions, that we begin to grasp something of the immensity of the mystery of the incarnation and Passion.

For the story has not ended. A eucatastrophe – to use Tolkien's rich image – lies around the corner, which we explore in *Resurrection*, another volume in this series. In anticipation of its themes, let us end with Richard Crashaw's divine epigram 'On the sepulchre of our Lord', which I shall quote in its pithy, succinct entirety:

> Here, where our Lord once laid his Head,
> Now the grave lies buried.

Lord, help us to trust you, even when we feel that you are not there and long for the consolation of your presence. May our Good Fridays become our Easter Day.

for further reading

Introductory

The following are suitable for those engaging with scholarly discussion of the nature
of redemption for the first time.

Dillistone, F. W., *The Christian Understanding of Atonement*. London: SCM Press,
    1984.
Gunton, Colin E., *The Actuality of Atonement*. Edinburgh: T. & T. Clark, 1988.
McGrath, Alister E., *Christian Theology: An Introduction*. 3rd edn. Oxford/
    Cambridge, Mass.: Blackwell Publishers, 2001.

More advanced
Baillie, D. M., *God was in Christ: An Essay in Incarnation and Atonement*. London:
    Faber & Faber, 1956.
Bond, Helen K., *Pontius Pilate in History and Interpretation*. Cambridge:
    Cambridge University Press, 2004.
Brümmer, Vincent, *Atonement, Christology, and the Trinity: Making Sense of
    Christian Doctrine*. Aldershot: Ashgate, 2005.
Feenstra, Ronald J. and Plantinga, Cornelius (eds), *Trinity, Incarnation, and
    Atonement*. Notre Dame, Ind.: University of Notre Dame Press, 1989.
Ferguson, Everett, *Doctrines of Human Nature, Sin, and Salvation in the Early
    Church*. New York: Garland Publishing, 1993.
Franks, R. S., *The Work of Christ: A Historical Study*. London/New York: Nelson,
    1962.
Green, E. M. B., *The Meaning of Salvation*. London: Hodder & Stoughton, 1965.
Grensted, L. W., *A Short History of the Doctrine of the Atonement*. Manchester:
    Manchester University Press, 1920.
Hengel, Martin, *The Atonement*. London: SCM Press, 1981.

Hill, Charles E. and James, Frank A., *The Glory of the Atonement: Biblical, Historical and Practical Perspectives.* Downers Grove, Ill.: Inter-Varsity Press, 2004.

Hooker, Morna D., *Not Ashamed of the Gospel: New Testament Interpretations of the Death of Christ.* Carlisle: Paternoster Press, 1994.

Koen, Lars, *The Saving Passion: Incarnational and Soteriological Thought in Cyril of Alexandria's Commentary on the Gospel according to St John.* Uppsala: Acta Universitatis Uppsaliensis, 1991.

Lyall, Francis, *Slaves, Citizens, Sons: Legal Metaphors in the Epistles.* Grand Rapids, Mich.: Zondervan, 1984.

Martin, Dale B., *Slavery as Salvation: The Metaphor of Slavery in Pauline Christianity.* New Haven, Conn.: Yale University Press, 1990.

Morris, Leon, *The Apostolic Preaching of the Cross.* Leicester: Inter-Varsity Press, 1965.

Schmiechen, Peter, *Saving Power: Theories of Atonement and Forms of the Church.* Grand Rapids, Mich.: Eerdmans, 2005.

Sykes, S. W. (ed.), *Sacrifice and Redemption.* Cambridge: Cambridge University Press, 1991.

Van Dyk, Leanne, *The Desire of Divine Love: John McLeod Campbell's Doctrine of the Atonement.* New York: Peter Lang, 1995.

Wainwright, Geoffrey, *For Our Salvation: Two Approaches to the Work of Christ.* Grand Rapids, Mich.: Eerdmans, 1997.

Wiederkehr, Dietrich, *Belief in Redemption: Concepts of Salvation from the New Testament to the Present Time.* London: SPCK, 1979.

illustrations

On the Lawn by Amedeo Bocchi (1883–1976), Aphel College, Rome, Italy, © 1990, Photo Scala, Florence – courtesy of the Ministero per i Beni e le Attività Culturali.

The Prodigal's Return by Sir Edward John Poynter (1836–1919), Private Collection, © The Fine Art Society, London, UK/Bridgeman Art Library.

Last Supper by Jacopo Bassano (1515–92), Galleria Borghese, Rome, Italy, © 1990, Photo Scala, Florence – courtesy of the Ministero per i Beni e le Attività Culturali.

The Taking of Christ (oil on canvas) by Michelangelo Caravaggio (1571–1610) (follower of), Private Collection, © Lawrence Steigrad Fine Arts, New York/Bridgeman Art Library.

Ecce Homo (oil on canvas) by Antonio Ciseri (1821–91), Galleria d'Arte Moderna, Florence, Italy, © 1990, Photo Scala, Florence – courtesy of the Ministero per i Beni e le Attività Culturali.

Christ of St John of the Cross, 1951 (oil on canvas) by Salvador Dalí (1904–89), Art Gallery and Museum, Kelvingrove, Glasgow, Scotland, © Glasgow City Council (Museums)/Bridgeman Art Library.

Pietà (X.006) (oil on canvas) by El Greco (1541–1614), Private Collection.